The La Parmigiana Cookbook

A Story of Food and Family

The Gambino Family with Phil Keith

Photography by Lindsay Morris, Lindsay Morris Photography, Sag Harbor , New York.
lindsaycmorris.com

Published by:
Peconic Bay Consulting
Southampton, NY
all rights reserved

For additional copies:
order from
phil.keith@optonline.net
or: Amazon.com
ISBN-13: 978-1490364735

Table of Contents

Message from the Author:

It has been my privilege to know the Gambinos and their wonderful restaurant, La Parmigiana, for over twenty years. We always look forward to being greeted by the enticing aromas emanating from their kitchen as we slip into one of our favorite tables. Or, perhaps, we do takeout: the stack of "pies" we have ordered over the years would probably exceed the height of your local cell tower. It's like coming home to Mom's cozy dining room and not having to do the dishes.

La Parmigiana is also family: There is, of course, the wonderful family who built and runs the business; but the customers are family, too, and all are warmly welcomed, from the littlest to the patriarchs. Tradition runs deep here, and it is felt as soon as you walk through the door.

When the Gambinos asked if I would be interested in helping them create this combination family history and cookbook, I couldn't say "no." I have been so well treated over the years that the task would only be appropriate payback. Mr. Gambino was a true pillar of the community and he deserves a tribute to his perseverance, generosity, and ecumenical spirit.

I am just the scribe here. What you will see and read over the following pages belongs to the Gambino Family. It is an account of their hard work, eventual success and their treasured dishes. It showcases a collection of recipes that have been, until now, family secrets. They are published in this book for the first time. I would also like to acknowledge the superbly talented Lindsay Morris for the wonderful photographs that adorn these pages.

The Gambino Family believes now is the time to pay homage to the founder of their feast. This book is dedicated as a testimonial to Celestino Gambino. In honoring "Papa," the family also hopes to thank their loyal customers and offer up a celebration of good food made well and consumed joyfully. On behalf of the Gambino Family and La Parmigiana, we invite you to "Mangia," and "Enjoy!"

Phil Keith
Southampton, NY 2013

Papa's Story

He was happily married and the father of seven children. He had a decent job—selling sewing machine equipment—but the economy was rocky and he was concerned about the future—and all those mouths to feed. Opportunities to improve his situation were tenuous, at best, and he had always believed that there was something more in store for his future. He pondered long and hard about what to do. He had two brothers who had emigrated to another country and started a very successful restaurant based on their native cuisine. Knowing of his ambitions to do more, the brothers invited him to join them even though he knew nothing about their business, had no money to risk, and didn't speak a word of the language of the country where his brothers worked.

Given all these daunting circumstances, would you uproot your entire family and move a continent away, to a totally foreign country, and start over with nothing? Could you? Celestino Gambino felt he had to take the risk and he did just that.

Born February 9, 1937, the son of a Sicilian farmer and his wife, Celestino grew up in a small village near Palermo. By 1973, he and his wife, Josephine, had seven children, five girls and two boys. He was 36 years old and facing an uncertain future when fate intervened. Brothers Peter and John, who owned the Baby Moon restaurant in Westhampton Beach, invited him to come and work with them.

Not knowing any English or the first thing about the restaurant business, he began behind the counter at Baby Moon, learning to make pizzas , pastas and speak a new language through total immersion. Soon thereafter, he packed up his entire family and moved them to Long Island. It was not easy for the family, at first. The kids were placed in new schools and had to catch up quickly while taking unfamiliar subjects in a totally new language. They all lived in a rented house with not much more than beds and a few chairs. Celestino, however, was rapidly adapting to the American lifestyle and his new profession, and things began to run more smoothly.

By the latter part of 1974, Celestino was ready to take another gamble. He had explored the area and settled his mind on opening a restaurant of his own. He picked Southampton Village. 'There was just something different about the village," he often said. 'It felt more like home."

He rented a space on Hampton Road in Southampton, near the Town Hall, and opened a small pizza parlor he named "La Parmigiana." Why that name? "Because it's about the cheese," he always said. "Everything we do is about the cheese." Serving only pizza and spaghetti, at first, his deft touch with both his pasta and his customers soon allowed him to expand to a much broader menu, add more floor space, and the classic restaurant we know now as "La Parm" came into being.

The restaurant's reputation and business grew year after year. Eventually, all seven of Celestino and Josephine's children would work there; and, today, even some of his grandchildren work at La Parm. Celestino built the business on promises he unfailingly kept and handshakes, his son Rudy said. "You probably couldn't do that today," Rudy muses, "But my dad did it. We never had any contracts, or a lot of paperwork. We became local people and we took care of our local suppliers and distributors. Dad paid every bill and honored every agreement. He even sent money back to Sicily to pay off old family debts. That's the kind of guy he was."

The clientele grew steadily and today is frequented by locals and celebrities alike. All are treated the same way—warmly, respectfully and cordially. Celestino had a standing rule: he would not disclose who his customers might be if they were "rich and famous" and he would not allow his family or staff to do so either. Everyone was equally welcome and equally anonymous.

There were a few "bad apple" customers, Rudy smiled when he told the stories, "And dad had no trouble tossing them out, but, you know, every one of them eventually came back, even if it was two or three years later. That's because everyone loved him and respected him."

As the years went by, the business prospered. Celestino was able to buy a home for his family in Southampton Village. He completely redid the large kitchen and dining room adding large windows for maximum light. He installed a commercial stove, a wood-burning oven and a huge marble table. The dining table had to be large so that all his children and grandchildren could sit together for a family meal. The entire clan would gather for dinner every Monday—the only day that the restaurant was closed.

As more of his family joined him in the business, Celestino was able to attend to other things that he loved to do. He was very involved with his church, Southampton's Sacred Hearts of Jesus and Mary. For over 30 years he made dinner every Sunday for all the priests assigned to the church. He loved being generous and he contributed without fanfare to many causes that were close to his heart, most of them associated with the church.

In recent years he was able to take the business in different directions and assisted by son Rudy he expanded into the wholesale world. He and Rudy opened up a line of signature olive oils and salad dressings with the King Kullen food chain.

An intensely private and quiet man, whose life was his family and his business, he was a constant presence around the restaurant. With his signature pipe, which was never far from his touch, he ruled a small and beautiful empire with love, tradition and grace. This strong and hard working man, who was never sick, uncharacteristically fell ill in 2009 and after consulting with the doctors and going through a series of tests, it was determined that he had cancer. He fought valiantly, undergoing extensive treatment. Even while seriously ill, he still insisted on being at work. Sadly, the cancer finally overwhelmed him and he passed away on July 1, 2010, at the age of 73.

Congressman Tim Bishop, who represents Southampton and the New York First Congressional District in Washington, was a close friend of the family. He said this about Celestino Gambino in a resolution he presented to the United States Congress on the 4th of July, 2010:

"Madame Speaker, I rise with sadness to mark the death of Celestino Gambino, proprietor of La Parmigiana Restaurant in Southampton, New York, and a beloved member of the community... Celestino Gambino always had time for people. He always took the time to listen and find a way to help, quietly and without fanfare. He was a gentleman, considerate and kind, and he was respected for that... The Gambino family is a shining example of the hard work, family love, and generosity of spirit that have made this country great. With the death of Celestino Gambino, we have lost a bit of Southampton, but we know that his family will carry on the traditions he established at the place he owned and operated for 36 years, and in them he will live on and we will be constantly reminded of the values for which he stood."

Celestino
Gambino

The Dapper Young Man

With Family
in Sicily

Celestino and Josephine

The Restaurant Today: Today, the restaurant remains much the same as established by Celestino Gambino. The décor is definitely family style, and photos and maps of Italy adorn the walls. A map of Sicily is featured prominently on the place mats. There are fresh flowers on the tables: Mr. Gambino would never allow artificial flowers. Since his passing, there are memorials to Celestino and many family pictures gracing the walls. His spirit still guides the entire clan and oversees the business.

Patrons can be seated in the main dining room; or, in season (April through October) on the patio at the rear of the restaurant. A very robust menu offers appetizers, pizzas, sandwiches, main dishes, and desserts. Beer and wine is also available. Attire is informal and children are always welcome.

No reservations are taken; but, if you have a large party (six or more) you can call ahead and get an approximate time for a seating. All credit cards are welcome as are cash and personal checks. The restaurant is closed on Mondays.

The back wall of the main room of the restaurant is dominated by a painting completed by a local artist, the late Dr. Jack Riggio. It shows a montage of images from the pizza preparation process at "La Parm." The central figure is Rudy Gambino, the master pizza maker, hard at work. The prices may have changed a little since this painting was completed but the quality has remained as high as ever.

Maria manages the food line

Most of the entrees are prepared along the "food line," which takes up a good portion of one interior wall in the main dining room. The basic sauces, the mounds of cheese, the fresh salads and the pizza dough are conjured up in the underground prep rooms. The final entrees are completed on the food line. In addition to providing a fascinating tableau of the restaurant in action, this is where the wonderfully pleasing aromas start their journeys to your olfactory senses.

Rudy crafts a "grandma" pizza.

The magic conjured up by the pizza makers begins near the pizza ovens. The preparation counters brim with enticing ingredients and mounds of pizza dough are at the ready. During the cooler months, and slower times, the front ovens in the main dining room are used. When the action heats up in the summer and the back patio is open, the ovens in the rear of the restaurant are fired up and placed in service. Over the course of a year, all these ovens—and the pizza makers—will conjure up something in the neighborhood of 30,000 "pies!"

Immediately inside the front door is La Parmigiana's extensive deli: Here is where you will find all sorts of delectable offerings: fresh cheeses, prosciutto, olives, home-made salads, cookies, and prepared desserts.

Salads can be made up for take-out in the deli and there are several shelves of retail products direct from Italy, including fresh pasta, fish filets, vinegars, canned tomatoes and more.

ANTIPASTO

Antipasto Celestino:

"At the end of a busy day in the restaurant, as the last customers were being served, Celestino would finally get a chance to sit down and take a break. This is the dish he would ask for."

Ingredients:

6-ounce wedge of imported Provolone cheese
6 slices of imported prosciutto
6 slices of sopressata salami, sliced thin
Sicilian green olives
black olives
6-ounce wedge of Bel Paesa cheese
4 slices of semolina bread

Directions:

Arrange all the ingredients on a favorite plate, with the bread nearby. Pour a glass of red wine. This dish will serve two; but, if you're having company, expand the ingredients accordingly. This antipasto can be served either as an appetizer or as a late night accompaniment to a good bottle of wine.

Preparation Time: 15 minutes

MELANZANE SICILIANA

Ingredients:

6 baby eggplants, peeled; sliced ½ inch thick
1 tsp. salt
½ cup La Parmigiana extra virgin olive oil
1 cup tomato sauce (see"Sauces")
8 leaves fresh basil
½ cup Pecorino Romano cheese, grated

Directions:

In a large pot of cold water, add the salt and all the slices of eggplant. Let the eggplant sit in the cold water for 15 minutes then drain.

In a large frying pan, heat the oil until hot but not smoking. Fry the eggplant slices until they are lightly brown on each side.

In a separate small pot, gently warm the tomato sauce.

On a large platter, pour in half the tomato sauce. Place the cooked eggplant slices on the sauce then pour the remaining tomato sauce evenly over the eggplant slices. Sprinkle the Romano cheese on top of the eggplant and add the basil leaves.

Preparation Time: 20 minutes

RICE BALLS WITH BEEF & PEAS

Ingredients:

2 Tbsp. La Parmigiana extra virgin olive oil
½ small yellow onion, minced
1 lb. of fresh ground beef
Small bunch of fresh parsley, minced
Salt & pepper to taste
2 ½ cups of frozen peas
1 14-oz. can San Marzano peeled tomatoes

2 ½ cups Arborio rice
1 stick butter
6 cups of chicken or beef broth
2 Tbsp. Parmigiano Reggiano
3 Tbsp. Romano cheese
2 envelopes of saffron

2 eggs, beaten
2 cups of bread crumbs

2 cups Canola oil, for frying

Side dish of marinara or tomato sauce (see "Sauces")

Directions:

Heat the olive oil in a large saucepan; add the onions, cook until softened, 3 to 4 minutes; add beef, parsley, salt & pepper, brown for 10 minutes, then add peas and peeled tomatoes, simmer over low heat.

Boil the rice with the butter and chicken (or beef) broth for 10 minutes, then add the two cheeses and saffron, stir, remove from the heat.

When the rice mixture is cool, form "tennis balls" (makes 9-10) then pull them apart and fill the middles with beef & peas. Re-form rice around the beef & peas.

Roll the finished balls in the eggs first, then the bread crumbs.

Heat enough canola oil in a large saucepan to half-submerge the rice balls. Dip the balls in the hot oil and cook until they are golden brown.

Dry the rice balls on paper towels; then serve warm with a side of marinara or tomato sauce.

Preparation Time: 1 hour

SHRIMP MARINARA

Ingredients:

½ cup of La Parmigiana extra virgin olive oil
4 small cloves of fresh garlic, coarsely chopped
16 large shrimp, peeled, de-veined
½ tsp. black pepper
2 Tbsps. of fresh Italian parsley, chopped
2 Tbsps. fresh basil, finely chopped
¼ cup of white wine
1 cup of marinara sauce

Directions:

Warm the olive oil over medium-high heat, being careful not to let the oil burn. Add the garlic, and sauté for one minute. Add the shrimp, black pepper, parsley, and basil, sauté for 5-7 minutes, until the shrimp pieces are opaque. Add the white wine, sauté for an additional 3 minutes then add the marinara sauce and heat until the mixture is warm.

You can serve the dish as an antipasto or as a meal. If you toss the shrimp marinara preparation with a pound of linguini, cooked al dente, you will have a splendid entrée.

Preparation Time: 30 minutes

SICILIAN CAPONATA

Ingredients:

1/2 cup La Parmigiana extra virgin olive oil
2 large eggplants peeled & cubed
1 celery stalk, chopped
2 oz. capers
8 green olives, pitted & halved
1 small white onion, chopped
2 oz. white vinegar
1 Tbsp. sugar
5 fresh basil leaves
1 cup tomato sauce
(see "Sauces")

Directions:

In a large frying pan, heat the olive oil until hot then fry the eggplant cubes until they are light brown. Add and sauté the celery, capers, olives and onion until the whole mixture is light brown. Add the vinegar and simmer until the vinegar evaporates. Add the sugar and basil; stir. Add the tomato sauce and simmer for 10 minutes. Add the eggplant pieces and cook for another 5 minutes; serve.

Preparation Time: 35 minutes

Sauces:

Bolognese Sauce

These sauces are the compliments to many of the dishes featured in this cookbook. They are listed here with their ingredients and directions on how to make them. If a recipe says "3 cups Marinara sauce;" or, "one cup pesto sauce," etc., you will find how to conjure up each sauce in this section:

Ingredients:

1 carrot, chopped
3 stalks of celery, chopped
1 medium white onion, chopped
1 cup La Parmigiana extra virgin olive oil
1 pound of fresh ground beef
1 tsp. salt
1 tsp. black pepper
1 tsp. nutmeg
1/2 cup fresh parsley, chopped
1/2 cup of red wine
1-16 oz can San Marzano crushed tomatoes
5 leaves of fresh basil

Directions:

In a blender, add the carrot, celery and onion with the olive oil and blend until creamy.

In a 3-quart pot, heat the olive oil mix over medium heat for 5 minutes; then add the beef, salt, pepper, nutmeg, and parsley. Sauté until the meat is brown then add the wine and cook 5 additional minutes. Add the tomatoes and fresh basil and continue to cook for 20 more minutes over low heat.

Preparation Time: 20 minutes

CALAMARI SAUCE

"Papa had a little Vespa scooter he rode for many years, all around town. He was supposed to wear a helmet, but he never did. The police stopped him many times for not wearing his helmet until one day, they just finally gave up."

Ingredients:

½ cup La Parmigiana extra virgin olive oil
1 fresh garlic clove, chopped
1 pound fresh calamari, cut into rings
2 Tbsps. fresh Italian parsley, chopped
a pinch of black pepper
1 tsp. crushed red pepper
½ cup white wine
1 cup marinara sauce (see "marinara sauce," following)
5 leaves of fresh basil

Directions:

In a large frying pan heat the olive oil and add the garlic and sauté until golden brown. Add the calamari, parsley, black pepper, red pepper; sauté over medium heat for 5 minutes. Add the white wine and cook another 15 minutes. Drain half the liquid then add the marinara sauce and fresh basil, simmer until warm. You may then serve and eat as is or toss with spaghetti.

Preparation Time: 30 minutes

FRUTTI DI MARE SAUCE

Ingredients:

½ cup La Parmigiana extra virgin olive oil
3 cloves fresh garlic, sliced
1 tsp. black pepper
1 tsp. crushed red pepper
2 Tbsps. fresh Italian parsley, chopped
2 Tbsps. fresh basil, chopped
16 large shrimp, cleaned
½ pound fresh mussels, cleaned
1 dozen local Little Neck clams, removed from the shell
½ lb. calamari, cut into bite sized pieces
1/2 cup white wine
1 cup marinara sauce (see "marinara sauce," following)

Directions:

In a large frying pan heat the olive oil, add the garlic and sauté until golden brown; add the black and red pepper, parsley, basil, shrimp, mussels, clams and calamari; cover and cook just until the mussels open. Add the white wine and cook for 5 minutes more. Add the marinara sauce and cook an additional 10 minutes. Sauce is now ready to serve. You can eat it as is or mix it with any type of pasta.

Preparation Time: 25 minutes

MARINARA SAUCE

Ingredients:

3 fresh garlic cloves, finely chopped
1 medium onion, chopped
½ stick of sweet butter
½ cup La Parmigiana extra virgin olive oil
2-16 oz cans of San Marzano peeled tomatoes
1 tsp. salt
1 tsp. black pepper
1 Tbsp. sugar
10 leaves of fresh basil

Directions:

In a 3-quart pot, sauté the garlic and the chopped onion in the olive oil and the half-stick of butter until the onion is opaque, about 5 minutes.

Open the 2 cans of peeled tomatoes, crush them, then stir them into the pot. Add the salt, pepper, sugar and basil leaves and let the sauce cook over medium heat for 20 minutes.

Preparation Time: 30 minutes

TOMATO SAUCE

Ingredients:

1 medium onion, chopped
1/2 cup La Parmigiana extra virgin olive oil
1 Tbsp. dried basil
1-16 oz. can San Marzano crushed tomatoes
1-16 oz. can San Marzano peeled tomatoes
1 tsp. salt
1 tsp. black pepper
½ tsp. garlic powder
1 Tbsp. sugar
4 leaves of fresh basil
1 cup Romano cheese, grated

Directions:

In a 3-quart pot, sauté the onion in the olive oil; add the dry basil. When the onion browns, add the two cans of tomatoes, stir. Add the salt, pepper, garlic powder, sugar and fresh basil. Cook over medium heat for 20 minutes, then add the cheese; stir well.

Preparation Time: 20 minutes

PESTO SAUCE

Ingredients:

1 large bunch of fresh basil; washed, dried, coarsely chopped
4 oz. pignoli nuts
4 oz. Romano cheese, grated
4 oz. Parmigiano cheese, grated
2 garlic cloves
½ cup La Parmigiana extra virgin olive oil
1 tsp. salt
1 tsp. pepper

Directions:

Place all the ingredients in a blender; blend until you have a paste.

To make a delicious entrée with this sauce, boil 1-pound of gnocchi; drain, and mix with the pesto.

Preparation Time: 10 minutes

(Fresh pesto sauce is one of the ready-made sauces available for purchase in the deli.)

SOUPS:

Chicken Soup:

Nothing warms you up better on a chilly day than a bowl of Italian soup. A great soup can also be the whole meal—with a loaf of fresh Italian bread, of course!

Ingredients:

1 whole, natural (organic) chicken, cut into 4 parts
1 stalk of celery, chopped
4 carrots, chopped
2 whole leeks, sliced thin
½ tsp. salt
1 tsp. black pepper
2 bay leaves
2 Tbsps. fresh basil, chopped
1 Tbsp. dried basil
2 cloves of garlic, crushed
½ cup fresh Italian parsley, chopped
1 cup La Parmigiana extra virgin olive oil
1 pound of pasta (couscous or small pasta)

Directions:

In a large pot with one gallon of water, place the 4 chicken parts with the celery, carrots, leeks, salt, pepper, bay leaves, fresh basil, fresh garlic, fresh parsley and olive oil. Bring to a slow boil, then simmer until the chicken is thoroughly cooked. Remove the chicken parts and de-bone all the chicken meat. Chop the chicken meat and put it back into the pot; add the pasta and cook for an additional 20 minutes; serve.

Preparation Time: 90 minutes

MINESTRONE

Ingredients:

½ cup white beans
½ cup kidney beans
½ cup dried peas
½ cup dry lentils
2 carrots, chopped
½ stalk celery, chopped
1 medium white onion,
chopped
1 14-oz. can San Marzano
crushed tomatoes
1 Tbsp. each salt, black
pepper, dried basil
1 cup fresh parsley, chopped
1 tsp. sugar
½ pound sliced mushrooms
1 cup fresh asparagus,
chopped
1 cup fresh spinach
2 medium zucchinis, chopped
½ lb. D'italia pasta, dry
1 cup La Parmigiana extra
virgin olive oil

Directions:

In a large soup pot place all
the beans, peas and lentils
with enough water to cover
them. Add the carrots, celery,
onion and the canned
tomatoes. Add the salt,
pepper, dried basil, parsley
and sugar. Bring to a boil,
then simmer for one hour or
until the beans are cooked.
Add the mushrooms,
asparagus, spinach, zucchini
and the pasta and cook for
another 20 minutes. Add the
olive oil and fresh basil, stir
and serve.

*Preparation Time: 2 hours,
including cooking time*

VEGETABLE LENTIL SOUP

Ingredients:

1 gallon of water
½ pound of dry lentils
1 small stalk of celery cut in small cubes
3 carrots, peeled & cut in small cubes
1 small white onion, finely chopped
1 small red onion, chopped
2 white potatoes cut into small cubes
1 tsp. salt
1 tsp. black pepper
3 garlic cloves, fresh, chopped
2 Tbsps. fresh Italian parsley, chopped
5 leaves of fresh basil
¼ cup La Parmigiana extra virgin olive oil
2 green zucchini, sliced thin
2 yellow zucchini, sliced thin
1 stalk of asparagus chopped small
1 cup of fresh spinach, chopped

Directions:

In a large pot, boil the water then add the lentils, celery, carrots, onions, potatoes, salt pepper, garlic, parsley, basil & olive oil: simmer for 30 minutes. Add the zucchini, asparagus, & spinach and simmer an additional 5 minutes. Serve, drizzling a little more olive oil on top.

Preparation Time: 50 minutes

SALADS:

GORGONZOLA SALAD

All of the hearty salads we feature here can be the meal, or a compliment to the meal. Be sure to serve with a basket of fresh Italian bread!

Ingredients:

1 head romaine lettuce, chopped coarsely
1 fresh tomato, sliced
2 oz. green Sicilian olives
2 oz. black olives
4 artichoke hearts
½ cup gorgonzola cheese
1 small red onion, sliced
¼ cup La Parmigiana Italian dressing

Directions:

Put the chopped romaine in a large salad bowl; add the tomato slices, olives, artichokes, cheese; place the onion slices on the top. Pour the dressing over the salad.

Preparation Time: 15 minutes

OCTOPUS SALAD

Ingredients:

water for boiling
2 pounds of fresh octopus
2 whole lemons
1 Tbsp. La Parmigiana extra virgin olive oil
1/2 stalk of celery, chopped
8 oz. of canned pimentos, chopped
1 Tbsp. of fresh Italian parsley, chopped
1 tsp. black pepper
1 tsp. salt

Directions:

In a pot of boiling water (enough to cover the octopus) boil the octopus for 20 minutes with one lemon, cut in half. After 20 minutes, turn off the heat and let the pot stand for another 20 minutes. Drain the octopus and cut into pieces.

In a large bowl, mix the cut pieces of octopus with all the other ingredients, then squeeze the juice of one lemon over all; serve.

Preparation Time: 1 hour

SEAFOOD SALAD

Ingredients:

2 quarts of water
1 tsp. salt
½ pound of calamari, cut into rings
3 small octopus, cut into bite sized pieces
½ pound of fresh mussels
10 medium shrimp, cleaned and de-veined
¼ pound of scallops
1 stalk of celery, chopped
1 small can of pimentos, diced
1 small bunch of Italian parsley, chopped
1 whole lemon (for juice)
1 tsp. black pepper
1 cup of La Parmigiana extra virgin olive oil
½ cup white vinegar
1 whole lemon, cut in wedges

Directions:

Bring two quarts of water to boil in a medium pot then add the salt, calamari and octopus: cook until soft (20 minutes), drain, and place in a large bowl.

In a steamer, steam the mussels just enough to make them open, drain them, toss them in the bowl with the calamari and octopus. Boil the shrimp and scallops for 10 minutes; drain, and toss them in with the rest of the seafood.

Put in the celery, pimentos, parsley; squeeze one lemon over all, sprinkle with pepper, then add the olive oil and vinegar. Toss everything well, decorate with the lemon wedges, then serve.

Preparation time: 30-40 minutes

Main Dishes:

CHICKEN PARMIGIANA:

These dishes are the main events. Over the years, since the opening of the restaurant, these selections have passed the test of time with our most loyal patrons—and our very particular family members. When we want to prepare a hearty dish to satisfy, these are the meats, the pasta dishes, and the seafood entrees we turn to again and again.

Ingredients:

8 chicken cutlets (about 1 pound)
1 cup Italian bread crumbs
2 eggs, beaten
1 cup soy bean oil
1 cup tomato sauce (see "Sauces")

Directions:

Heat the oven to 400 degrees. Coat each cutlet in the eggs, then the bread crumbs. In a large frying pan, heat the oil over medium-high heat (but don't let the oil smoke). Cook each cutlet in the hot oil until golden brown. Remove cutlets from the oil and place them in a baking dish. Cover the cutlets with the tomato sauce and lay mozzarella cheese on top. Bake the dish at 400 degrees just until the cheese is melted, serve.

Preparation Time: 30 minutes

CHICKEN SCALOPPINI

Ingredients:

Broth:1/2 cup Marsala wine
2 Tbsp. salted butter
2 Tbsp. white flour
2 cups of water
2 chicken broth cubes

Flour Mix:
1/2 cup white flour
1 tsp. salt
1 tsp. black pepper
1 tsp. sage
1 tsp. nutmeg
½ tsp. garlic powder

6 thin chicken cutlets
½ cup of La Parmigiana extra virgin olive oil for cooking
4 oz. dry porcini mushrooms¼ cup fresh parsley, chopped

Directions:

Broth: In a stock pot, boil the water and chicken broth cubes. In a sauce pan, heat the alcohol until it is burned, then add the broth. Add the butter until melted then add the flour a little at a time to make a paste.

Flour Mix: Mix all the ingredients together in a bowl. Coat each slice of chicken in the flour mix. Heat the oil then cook each slice for 2 minutes. Add the Marsala mix and the mushrooms, cook for 5 more minutes.

Sprinkle some chopped parsley on top; serve.

Preparation Time: 30 minutes

EGGPLANT PARMIGIANA

Ingredients:

2 large eggplants, peeled ½ inch thick
cold water to cover and soak the eggplant slices
1 tsp. of salt
2 eggs, beaten
1 cup Italian seasoned bread crumbs
1 cup frying oil
1 cup of tomato sauce (see "Sauces")
8 slices of mozzarella cheese
¼ cup Romano cheese, grated

Directions:

Heat the oven to 375 degrees. Cut the peeled eggplants into half-inch thick slices. Soak the eggplant slices in cold water and the salt for ten minutes, drain and dry them. Coat the slices in the eggs then the bread crumbs. In a large frying pan, heat the oil (but don't let it smoke), then cook the coated eggplant slices until they are golden brown. In a baking dish, cover the bottom of the dish with half the tomato sauce. Place the cooked eggplant slices on top of the sauce. Pour the remaining sauce over the eggplant. Lay the mozzarella slices on top of the eggplant and sauce. Put the dish in the pre-heated oven and bake until the mozzarella is completely melted, serve.

Preparation Time: 40 minutes

FARFALLE WITH CHERRY TOMATOES, ASPARAGUS, SHRIMP & GRILLED CHICKEN

"The seven of us, growing up, our curfew every night, even on weekends was eleven o'clock. Papa would go from room to room, making sure we were all in bed. And we were, except sometimes for Rudy. Rudy would wait until Papa had checked on all of us then he'd sneak out, roll the car down the driveway in neutral so Papa wouldn't hear the motor."

Ingredients:

½ cup La Parmigiana extra virgin olive oil
3 garlic cloves, chopped½ pint fresh cherry tomatoes, cut in half
4 large shrimp, cleaned & de-veined
15-20 fresh asparagus tips
8-oz. grilled chicken, cubed
1 tsp. salt
1 tsp. pepper
10 leaves of fresh basil
½ pound farfalle pasta
2 Tbsps. Romano cheese, grated

Directions:

In a frying pan, heat the olive oil, then add the garlic, cherry tomatoes, shrimp, asparagus, chicken, salt, pepper, fresh basil and sauté for 10 minutes.

In a large pot, cook the farfalle pasta per the instructions; drain. Add the sauté mix to the pasta, sprinkle the Romano cheese on top; serve.

Preparation Time: 20 minutes

FETTUCCINI PARMIGIANA

Ingredients:
4 Tbsp. butter
1 small onion, chopped small
1 small basket of fresh mushrooms, sliced10 slices of boiled ham, cut into 1 inch pieces
2 Tbsps. of fresh Italian parsley, chopped fine
1 tsp. black pepper
½ pound of fettuccini pasta
1 tsp. salt
1 cup heavy cream
2 Tbsp. Romano cheese, grated

Directions:

In a large pot melt the butter, with the onion; add sliced mushrooms, ham, parsley and pepper; sauté for 10 minutes on low heat.

In another large pot, cook the fettuccini per the instructions, with the salt until soft; drain.

Add the cooked pasta to the ham mix; add the heavy cream and cheese and mix until creamy; serve.

Preparation Time: 30 minutes

FUSILLI SICILIAN STYLE

Ingredients:

1/2 cup La Parmigiana extra virgin olive oil
3 cloves fresh garlic, chopped
1 Tbsp. capers
2 anchovies, sliced thin
½ cup Gaeta olives, pitted
½ cup Sicilian green olives, pitted
1 Tbsp. Italian parsley, chopped
1 16-oz. can peeled tomatoes
10 leaves fresh basil
1 tsp. black pepper
1 Tbsp. sugar
1 pound fusilli pasta
2 Tbsps. grated Romano cheese

Directions:

Heat the olive oil in a large frying pan over medium-high heat, then add chopped garlic, capers, anchovies, olives & parsley; sauté for 10 minutes. Add the peeled tomatoes, basil, black pepper & sugar; cook for 15 minutes over low heat.

In a large pot, cook the pasta per the directions, with the salt, until soft; drain.

Add cooked pasta to the mixture, sprinkle with the cheese, serve.

Preparation Time: 40 minutes

LASAGNA

Ingredients:

1 12-oz. container of Polly-O ricotta cheese
6 slices of boiled ham, sliced thin, then chopped

1 tsp. dried parsley
1 tsp. black pepper
4 cups of water
1 tsp. La Parmigiana extra virgin olive oil
1 pound box of lasagna pasta
1 cup Bolognese sauce (see "Sauces")
1 cup tomato sauce (see "Sauces")
8 slices of fresh mozzarella

Directions:

Heat the oven to 375 degrees.
In a large bowl, mix the ricotta with the chopped ham, parsley, and black pepper; put aside. In a large pot, boil the water with the olive oil. Place the lasagna pasta in the boiling water and cook until soft then drain.

In a large oven dish, place half the Bolognese sauce on the bottom, then place a layer of pasta (one third) on top of the sauce. Spread the ricotta mixture on top of the first layer, then add the rest of the Bolognese sauce. Add a second layer of pasta (the next third) on top of the ricotta mix; cover with half the tomato sauce. Add the final layer of pasta and the second half of the tomato sauce.

Bake in the oven for 20 minutes, then add the mozzarella evenly over the top. Return to the oven for 5 minutes or until the mozzarella is completely melted. Remove from the oven, slice and serve.

Preparation Time: 1 hour

LINGUINI WITH WHITE CLAM SAUCE

"Nonno didn't like my skateboard. he was always afraid I was really going to hurt myself. One day, he pulled $300 dollars out of his pocket and offered to buy my skateboard, right then and there."

Ingredients:

½ cup La Parmigiana extra virgin olive oil
5 cloves of fresh garlic, chopped
1 tsp. black pepper
1 tsp. crushed red pepper
1 small bunch of fresh Italian parsley, chopped
2 dozen local Little Neck clams, removed from the shells
½ pound of linguini pasta

Directions:

In a large frying pan sauté the garlic in the olive oil until the garlic is golden brown: add the black pepper, red pepper and parsley; stir, then add the clams. Cook over medium heat for 5 minutes.

In a separate large pot, cook the linguini as directed, until al dente; drain, then put in a large bowl. Pour the clam mixture over the top of the pasta, serve.

Preparation Time: 25 minutes

MARGARITA MELANZANE

"This was one of my father's favorite dishes. You could catch him almost every night, in summertime, sitting outside enjoying this dish, after which he would peacefully smoke his pipe. This was the quiet, thoughtful and soothing state of mind he always portrayed."

Ingredients:

3 baby eggplants; peeled, sliced 1 inch thick
cold water (enough to cover the eggplant)
1 Tbsp. salt
½ cup La Parmigiana extra virgin olive oil
2 cups tomato sauce (See "Sauces")
4 cups water
½ pound of marguerite pasta
½ cup Pecorino Romano cheese, grated
6 leaves fresh basil, chopped

Directions:

Put the peeled and sliced eggplants in a bowl with the cold water and salt. Immerse the slices for 10 minutes, drain.

In a frying pan heat the olive oil, add the eggplant slices and fry on each side until golden brown; add the tomato sauce.

In a separate pot, cook the pasta per the directions until soft, then drain. Put the pasta in the sauce and eggplant mix. Add the cheese and basil and serve.

Preparation Time: 30 minutes

MEAT BALLS

This is the classic La Parmigiana meat ball recipe.

Ingredients:

1 pound of fresh ground beef1 egg, beaten
½ cup of Italian bread crumbs
½ cup of milk
1 tsp. salt
1 tsp. black pepper
1 cup fresh Italian parsley, chopped
1 cup grated Romano cheese
½ cup grated mozzarella cheese
1 tsp. garlic powder
½ cup tomato sauce (see *"Sauces"*)

Directions:

Pre-heat the oven to 375 degrees. In a large bowl, mix everything together with your hands until well blended. Take an ice cream scoop and make balls using all the mixture. Place each ball on a flat baking tray. Put a little water in the bottom of the tray, just enough to cover the surface of the tray.

Put the meatballs in the oven and bake for 30 minutes.

Heat the tomato sauce and pour over the meatballs as you serve them.

Preparation Time: 50 minutes

MUSSELS MARINARA

Ingredients:

½ cup La Parmigiana extra virgin olive oil
5 cloves fresh garlic, chopped
1 Tbsp. butter
2 Tbsp. fresh Italian parsley, chopped
5 leaves of fresh basil
1 tsp. crushed red pepper
2 pounds of fresh mussels, cleaned
1/2 cup white wine
1 cup marinara sauce (see "Sauces")

Directions:

In a large frying pan heat the olive oil, add the garlic and sauté until golden brown. Add the butter, parsley, basil, red pepper and stir then add the mussels and cover the pan. Cook over medium heat just until the mussels open (about 10 minutes) then add the wine. Cook 5 minutes more, until the wine evaporates. Add the marinara sauce, cook another 5 minutes then serve.

Preparation Time: 30 minutes

ORECCHIETTE, SAUSAGE & BROCCOLI RABE

"Orecchiette" is a type of pasta usually associated with southern Italy: it's name comes from its shape; which, in Italian, translates into "little ears." In this dish, however, when combined with the sausage and fresh broccoli rabe, it becomes a feast for another sense: taste!

Ingredients:

2 oz. La Parmigiana extra virgin olive oil
1 clove fresh garlic, coarsely chopped
1 lb. of Italian sausage,* sliced
1 tsp. black pepper
1 tsp. crushed red pepper
2 oz. white wine
2 quarts of. water
1 tsp. salt
2 heads of broccoli rabe
½ pound of Orecchiette pasta
2 Tbsps. grated Romano cheese

*You can use sweet sausage; or, if you like your pasta a little more spicy, you can also use hot sausage.

Directions:

In a large frying pan, heat the olive oil and sauté the garlic until brown; add the sausage, black and red pepper and white wine. Cook until the sausage is browned.

In a separate pot, bring 2 quarts of water with the salt to a boil, add the broccoli rabe, and cook for 5 minutes; drain.

In a large bowl, combine hot broccoli rabe and sausage mix and stir it all together. In a pot of 2 quarts of boiling water, cook the orecchiette, drain, and mix into the broccoli rabe and sausage; add the Romano cheese, toss, then serve.

Preparation Time: 30 minutes

ORECCHIETTE WITH VEAL BOLOGNESE & PEAS

Ingredients:

½ cup La Parmigiana extra virgin olive oil
1 small white onion, chopped
1 pound of ground veal
pinch of salt & pepper
6 leaves fresh basil, chopped
1/2 cup canned baby peas
2 oz. red wine
1 12-oz can San Marzano crushed tomatoes
1 pound orecchiette pasta
½ cup Romano cheese, grated
1 Tbsp. sugar

Directions:

In a frying pan, heat half the olive oil, sauté the onion until brown.

In a large pot, heat the remaining olive oil and when hot, add cooked onion, veal, a pinch of salt, a pinch of pepper and the basil. Sauté for 10 minutes then add the peas and the wine; cook over low heat for 10 minutes. Add the crushed tomatoes, let simmer for 15 minutes.

In a separate pot, cook the pasta per the directions with the salt; drain, then add to the veal mixture and stir. Place the pasta on a large serving platter and sprinkle with the Romano cheese.

Preparation Time: 50 minutes

PENNE NORCINA

Ingredients:

1/2 cup La Parmigiana extra virgin olive oil
1 lb. fresh, ground pork
½ cup sliced mushrooms
1 small yellow onion, chopped
1 tsp. dried sage
1 tsp. black pepper
1 Tbsp. fresh Italian parsley, chopped
1/4 cup dry, red wine
¼ cup heavy cream
1 cup marinara sauce (see "Sauces")
1 pound of penne pasta
1 tsp. salt
1 Tbsp. grated Romano cheese
Several leaves fresh basil, coarsely chopped

Directions:

With half the olive oil, brown the pork in a frying pan. In a separate large pot, sauté the mushrooms and the onion with the remaining olive oil for 5 minutes then add the pork, sage, black pepper and parsley. Add the wine and sauté another 5 minutes; add the cream and marinara sauce and simmer for 20 minutes.

Boil the pasta per the directions with the salt; drain. Add the cooked pasta to the pork mixture. Transfer the penne and pork to a serving dish, sprinkle with the Romano cheese, add some fresh basil, serve.

Preparation Time: 45 minutes

PENNE VODKA

"My dad did so many things in his quiet way, people never knew. A homeless veteran showed up. My dad put him to work, even got him a place to live. He worked for us for a long time then, sadly, he passed away. He had no family. Dad made his funeral arrangements and paid for everything out of his own pocket. He said it was the right thing to do."

Ingredients:

3 Tbsp. salted butter
1/2 cup vodka
1 cup heavy cream
½ cup tomato sauce (see "Sauces")
10 leaves of fresh basil, chopped
Pinch of black pepper
4 cups of water
1 tsp. salt
1 pound penne pasta
2 Tbsp. Romano cheese, grated

Directions:

In a large frying pan melt the butter on low heat, add the vodka; sauté for 10 minutes. Add the heavy cream, tomato sauce, basil, and a pinch of black pepper; cook for 10 more minutes on low heat.

In a separate large pot, boil the water and the salt; add the pasta and cook for 15 minutes; drain. Add the tomato mix to the pasta, stir in the Romano cheese.

[Note: chunks of cooked chicken are a nice touch if you want to add some meat to this dish.]

Preparation Time: 30 minutes

RIGATONI SPRING STYLE

Ingredients:

4 Tbsp. butter
8 slices of ham, sliced thin, then chopped into small pieces
8 slices of pancetta, chopped
1 Tbsp. fresh Italian parsley, chopped
1 tsp. black pepper
2 oz. canned sweet baby peas
1 pound of large rigatoni pasta
1 cup heavy cream
2 Tbsp. grated Romano cheese

Directions:

In a pan, melt the butter over medium high heat then cook the chopped ham, pancetta, parsley, and black pepper for 15 minutes; add the peas and cook for 5 minutes more, then set aside.

In a large pot, cook the rigatoni per the directions, for 15 minutes; then drain. Add the ham and pancetta mix plus the heavy cream and grated cheese. Mix and cook for 5 more minutes over low heat; serve.

Preparation Time: 45 minutes

SPAGHETTI CARBONARA

Ingredients:

1 stick of salted butter
2 slices, ½ inch thick, pancetta cut into cubes
10 slices of boiled ham, sliced into 1-inch cubes
2 Tbsp. Italian parsley, chopped
1 tsp. black pepper
3 cups of water
1 pound spaghetti
1 tsp. salt
1 cup heavy cream
1 egg yolk
½ cup Parmigiano cheese, grated

Directions:

In a large frying pan, melt the butter and add the bacon, sauté one minute, then add the ham, parsley and black pepper; sauté another 10 minutes, set aside.

In a large pot, cook the spaghetti in boiling water with the salt until al dente; drain.

Add the pasta to the bacon and ham then add the cream and the egg yolk and stir quickly, not allowing the egg yolk to cook, then sauté for another 5 minutes. Add the cheese and stir until well mixed, serve.

Preparation Time: 30 minutes

Desserts:

TIRAMISU:

Here are our best finishing touches: the deserts that we serve our friends and family. They are the perfect compliments to the end of the feast.

Ingredients:

3 egg yolks
1/2 cup sugar
1 lb. mascarpone cheese
3 egg whites

2 cups of espresso
¼ cup Kahlua
24 lady fingers

2 Tbsps. cocoa powder

Directions:

Beat the egg yolks with the sugar until smooth; add the mascarpone to the egg yolk mix and blend by hand. Beat the egg whites until creamy, then carefully blend, by hand, with the mascarpone and egg yolk mix.

In a separate bowl, mix the espresso and the Kahlua. Dip the lady fingers in the espresso mix and then lay down a layer of eight lady fingers in the bottom of a square pan or glass baking dish.

Cover the first layer of lady fingers with the egg and mascarpone mix, using about one third of the mix. Add the second layer of lady fingers and one-third more of mix.
Add the third layer and the last of the mix. Dust the top layer with the cocoa powder then refrigerate for 2 hours before serving.

Preparation time: 30 minutes (plus 2 hours refrigeration time)

CANNOLIS

"Nonno was the best. When we were little kids we'd show up at the restaurant and he'd pull $50 dollars out of his pocket and say, 'Here, go get ice cream.' Fifty dollars for ice cream! That was a lot of money for ice cream, and for us young kids! But there were a lot of us."

Ingredients:

1 pound Impastata ricotta
½ cup chocolate chips
¼ cup confectioner's sugar
¼ cup crème de cacao
6 cannoli shells

Directions:

In a large bowl, stir together the ricotta, chocolate chips, sugar and cocoa, mixing well.

Stuff each cannoli shell with one-sixth of the mix; sprinkle with a little more confectioner's sugar.

Preparation Time: 30 minutes

PIZZA

At La Parmigiana, pizza was there at the beginning. Consistently voted "The Best Pizza in the Hamptons" by any number of newspapers, magazines, critics, and websites, every single pizza served in the restaurant is made at the time it is ordered and from fresh ingredients only.

Rudy Prepares Another "Pie"

The dough is prepared on site as is the pizza sauce. The cheese, grated daily, comes from a trusted partner who has been with the family since the first pizzas came out of the oven. The plain cheese pie is the most requested pizza, but there are more than two dozen other toppings available, from meatballs, pepperoni, and grilled chicken to broccoli, spinach and eggplant. La Parmigiana also offers a gluten free pizza, white pizza , and several other gourmet pizzas. In recent years, the restaurant has added a "grandma pizza," square in shape; a marguerite type pizza whose popularity has soared.

The busy staff and highly productive pizza ovens turn out an amazing 30,000 pizzas a year. Recently, Rudy has been offering a line of frozen pizzas that are being distributed in the tri-state area.

The business prepares a thousand frozen pizzas a week, all sold before they go out the door. The next goal of 5,000 frozen pizzas a week will be within reach when Rudy finishes his plans for an off-site food preparation and packaging operation, which will be set up locally.

OLIVE OILS, DRESSINGS & SAUCES

Fresh, first press olive oil has always been essential to the recipes used in the restaurant. It was also, for Celestino, a touch of home. It was only natural, then, for Celestino to want to give his customers a taste of the oil he used; so, soon after La Parmigiana opened its doors, the family began a separate but complementary olive oil distribution business.

Every drop of La Parmigiana's signature olive oil comes from the finest olive trees in southern Sicily. Rudy tells the story of how the oil was handled in the early days of the operation:

"Twice a year we would get a container of fresh oil, and when I say 'container,' I'm talking about a truck pulling up to dad's house in Southampton towing a twenty by forty foot storage container. It was packed with pallets containing huge bottles of fresh olive oil. We would spend a whole night unloading half the container into Dad's basement.

"Then the next day, we'd unload the other half of the container into the basement at my grandma's house. For many nights after each delivery, the whole family would be up late and bottling fresh olive oil. A shipment would last us about six months, then we'd start all over again as soon as a new container arrived. It was quite a circus!"

To honor their patriarch, recently re-designed labels are on the bottles: they feature a silhouette of Celestino in his signature cap, with his ever-present pipe.

Proprietary bottled salad dressings from La Parmigiana are another featured product. Several formulations are available and for sale at the restaurant and at local King Kullen stores, Wild By Nature outlets, a few specialty stores and selected farm stands. To go along with the frozen pizza business, and to complement the home preparation of any of a number of the recipes featured in this book, La Parmigiana also offers a number of its sauces for retail sale. Olive oil, dressings, fresh pasta, sauces and frozen pizzas can all be ordered on line at: http://www.foodiesgourmet.com/la-parmigiana-specialties/.

Soon after expanding his initial menu of pizza and spaghetti, Celestino had the ambition to offer a line of retail groceries to his customers. He wanted to emphasize good food and specialty products that his clientele could not get elsewhere.

Today, the main retail operation resides on the deli side of the restaurant where shoppers can find a highly selective line of Italian food products, most of which are featured in the restaurant's signature dishes.

The pastas are fresh and vacuum sealed in Italy. The tomato products are mostly from the Strianese brand, also from Italy. Browse the shelves and you will find dried beans, jarred fish fillets, canned tuna, peppers, mushrooms and more. For those with a sweet tooth there are a number of confectionery products and chocolates. A large cold case stocks bottled water, sodas, fruit beverages and many perishable offerings, most with an Italian theme.

TAKE-OUT AND CATERING:

Anything on the menu can be ordered for take-out. Most popular, of course, are the pizzas, followed by signature sandwiches (like the large meatball heroes) and several main dishes that are requested over and over. Catering is available for parties and special events.

La Parmigiana

The start of a traditional family dinner at the Gambino's Southampton home

Surveying some of the dinner "guests."

A family favorite is rice balls--some with cheese, some with beef and peas. In this photo, Josephine has a batch in the cooking oil, above, and a plate ready to eat.

The finished product--absolutely delicious, and not to be missed.
How many can you eat?

Once the octopus is cooked, Frank makes the final preparations (top)
Rudy prepares some giant prawns (from Cor-J Seafood) and then they go right on the grill
(bottom)

Josephine prepares "spadini," which starts with thinly sliced steak, breadcrumbs, raisins, and pignoli nuts. The slices of steak are covered with the spadini mix, then rolled, and skewered. The spadini Josephine is holding are ready for the barbecue.

From the grill, expertly cooked by Rudy, comes the octopus, spadini and the prawns. With salad, pasta, and rice balls we are ready for everyone to dig in.

From left to right, sisters Maria, Rosie, Anna, and Joanne share a light moment before dinner.

While Rudy works the barbecue, Phil and Laura "grill" the grandkids for stories about Grandpa.

Everything is finally ready, and we're all invited to share the feast.

"Places everyone! Who's going to say grace?"

There is not a better, warmer, more bounteous, or inviting table in all the Hamptons than the one at the Gambino home. "Buon Appetito!"

ACKNOWLEDGMENTS:

The family of Celestino Gambino would like to gratefully acknowledge the wonderful support of their many customers and friends. Starting with a small pizza parlor in 1974, the extended "family" of La Parmigiana has grown steadily over the years and now reaches all corners of the Hamptons as well wherever those who have patronized the restaurant have gone. We could not have succeeded without all of you who have tried our menus and decided you liked what we had to offer. We pledge to carry on in the spirit of the wonderful man who was and will forever be, the "Founder of our Feast."

We would also like to thank our many faithful suppliers and partners: DiCarlo Foods, Peter's Fruit Company, Adam Lowney, Cor-J Seafood, North Sea Plumbing and Noble Electricians, in particular. Many of you have been with us since the beginning and are with us still. Celestino always believed that a man was only as good as his word and his reputation. He always accepted a handshake as being as good as a written contract, and strove to keep every promise and all his obligations; but, we could not have done it--and he could not have done it--without your reciprocating support.

We would also like to thank our many friends in the community who are part of the governance of our wonderful Town and Village of Southampton. Celestino arrived in Southampton Village with a dream and not much more, but he immediately felt "at home." This was due, certainly, to the many town and village officials that made us feel welcome and were willing to give a total stranger and his family a warm welcome and a fair shake. The family is particularly grateful for our marvelous police professionals and the volunteer fire fighters and ambulance workers who keep our village safe.

We would also like to mention how much Celestino loved the comfort and blessings he and all of us received from the clergy and parishioners of the Sacred Hearts of Jesus and Mary Church--now a beautiful Basilica. Over the years and all the wonderful priests who have come to serve the community and our family, Celestino always found hope and solace in his church, and he tried very hard to give back in kind.

In 2014 we will celebrate our 40th year in business. As we look ahead to the future, we pledge to continue to serve you as best as we can. We are and always will be a local, family operation. We are not ambitious to expand or open additional restaurants. "Papa" would not approve of that approach. It was his goal to do all that he could, in this one location, to serve his community and support his family to the best of his abilities. That's what we wish to do, too, and we hope that all of you will continue, with us, on the wonderful journey that our dear"Papa" and "Nonno" started all those years ago.

Thank you, again, from the bottom of our hearts.

The Gambino Family

Notes: